Animals &ME

Pigs and Me

Sarah Harvey

Explore other books at:
WWW.ENGAGEBOOKS.COM

VANCOUVER, B.C.

e ⟶ WWW.ENGAGEBOOKS.COM

Pigs and Me
Animals and Me
Harvey, Sarah N., 1950 –
Edited by: A.R. Roumanis
Text © 2022 Engage Books
Design © 2022 Engage Books

Text set in GelPenUpright

FIRST EDITION / FIRST PRINTING

LIBRARY AND ARCHIVES CANADA CATALOGUING IN PUBLICATION

Title: Pigs and me / by Sarah Harvey
Names: Harvey, Sarah N., 1950- author
Description: Series statement: Animals and me

Identifiers: Canadiana (print) 20220395357 | Canadiana (ebook) 20220395365
ISBN 978-1-77476-684-2 (hardcover)
ISBN 978-1-77476-685-9 (softcover)
ISBN 978-1-77476-686-6 (epub)
ISBN 978-1-77476-687-3 (pdf)

Subjects:
LCSH: Swine—Juvenile literature.
LCSH: Swine—Behavior—Juvenile literature.
LCSH: Human behavior—Juvenile literature.

Classification: LCC SF395.5 .H37 2022 | DDC J636.4—DC23

This project has been made possible in part by the Government of Canada.

Canada

What do you
know about pigs?

3

Some pigs live on farms.

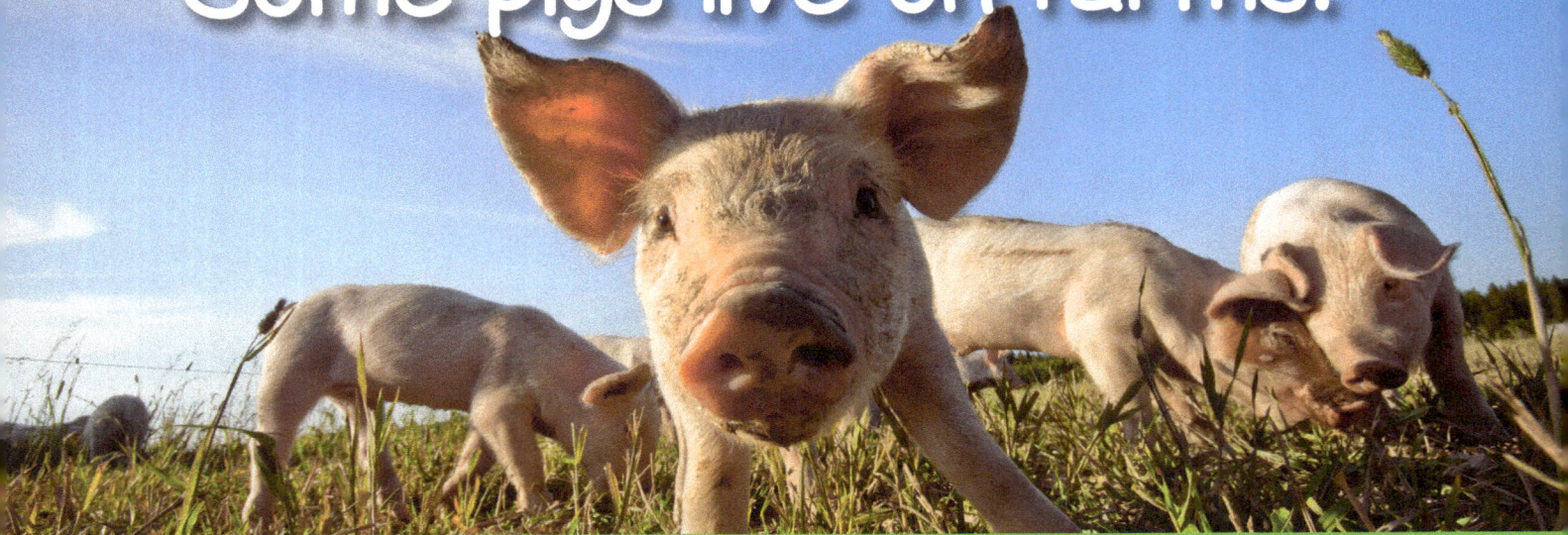

Some pigs live in the wild.

4

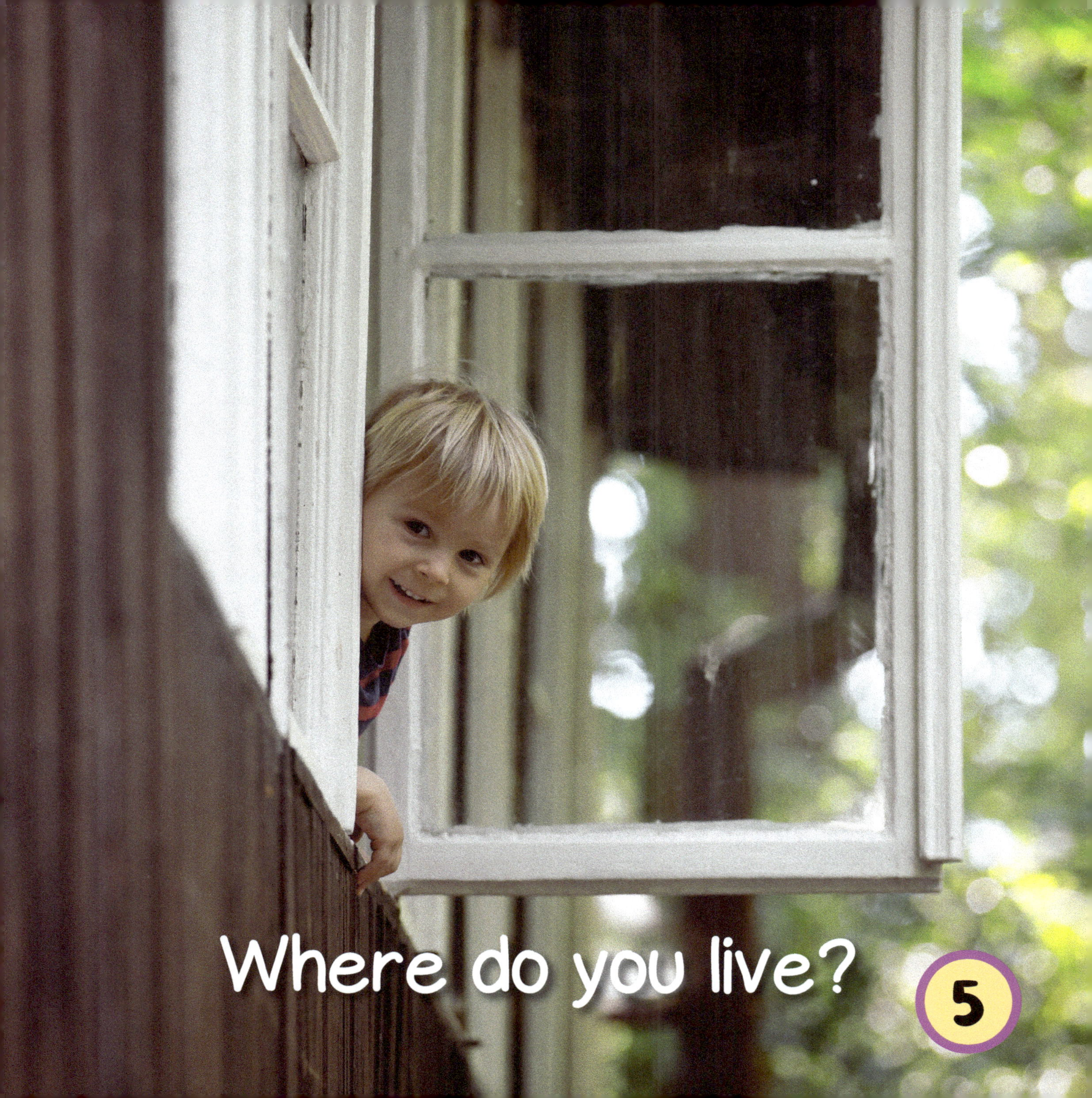

Where do you live?

Baby pigs are called piglets. They have lots of brothers and sisters.

Do you have brothers and sisters?

Piglets like to sleep close to each other.

How do you like to sleep?

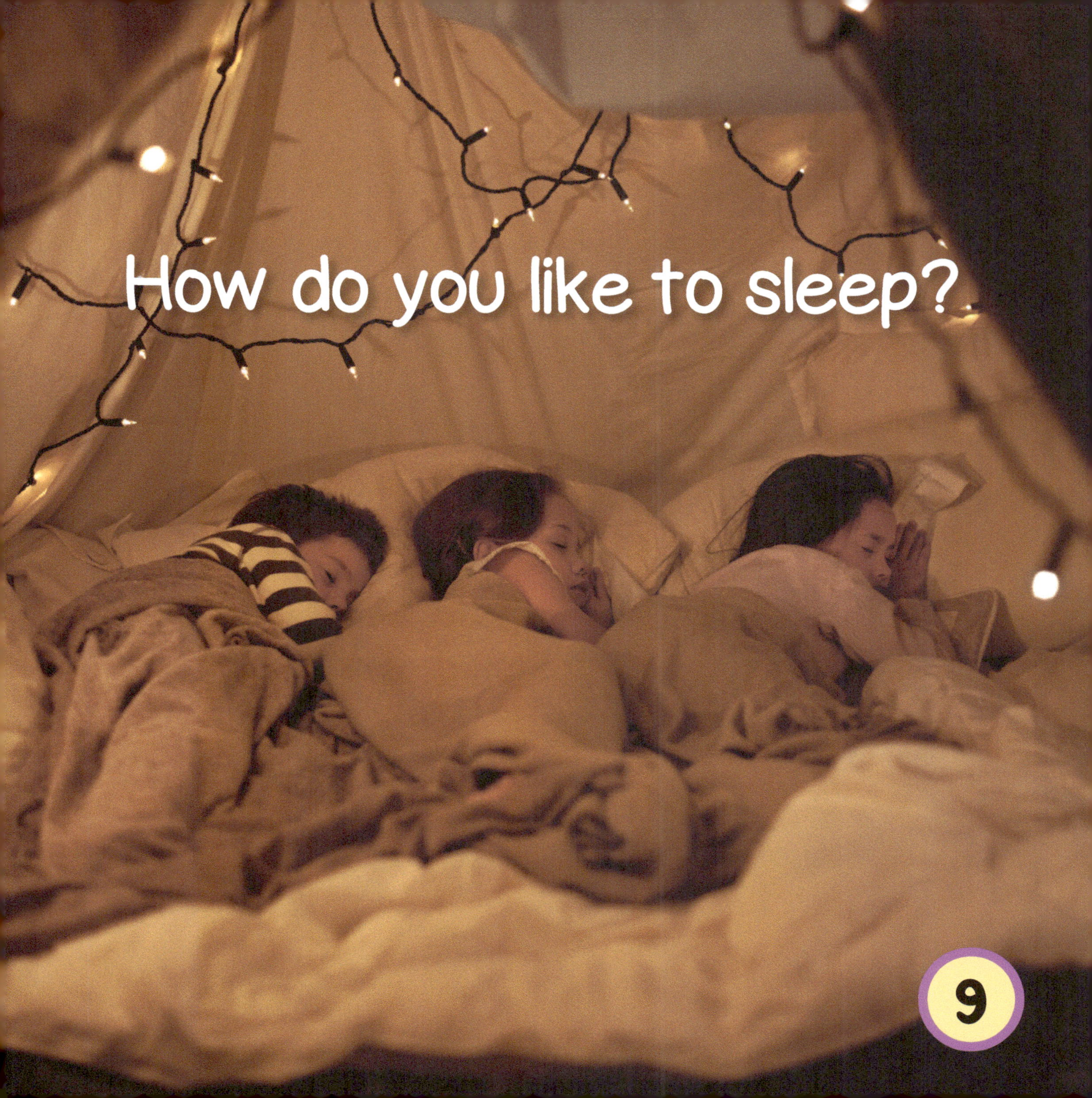

Farm pigs love to eat plants like corn or carrots. Wild pigs munch on fruit, roots, and leaves.

What's your favorite food?

11

Pigs talk by grunting.
Oink oink!

Who do you like to talk to?

13

Pigs love to roll in the mud to cool off.

14

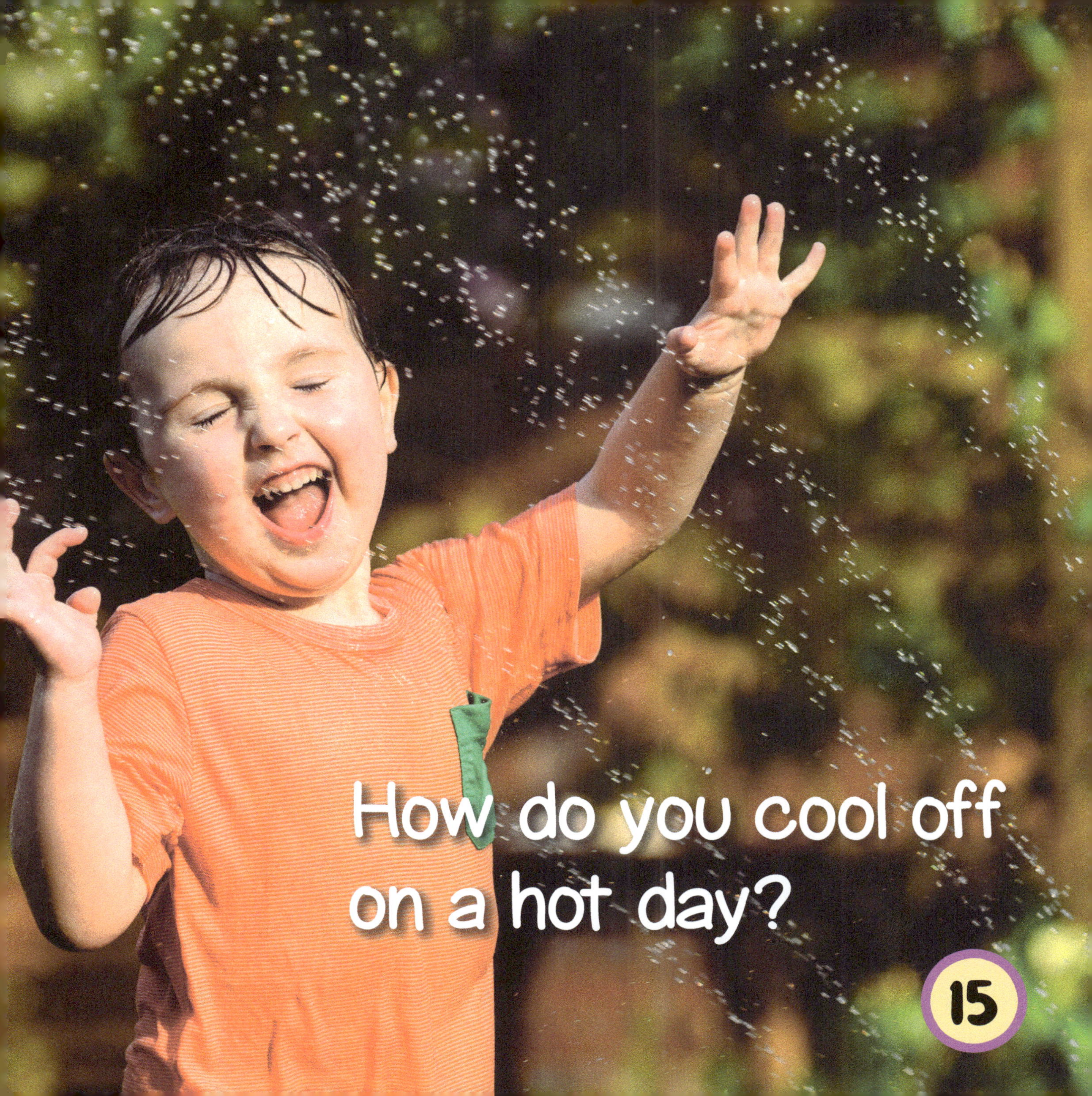

How do you cool off on a hot day?

Pigs dig up dirt with their noses.

Do you like to dig in the dirt?

Pigs have four toes but they only walk on two.

Can you walk on your toes?

Pigs have a very good sense of smell.

What's your favorite smell?

21

Piglets like to play with their friends.

Who do you like
to play with?

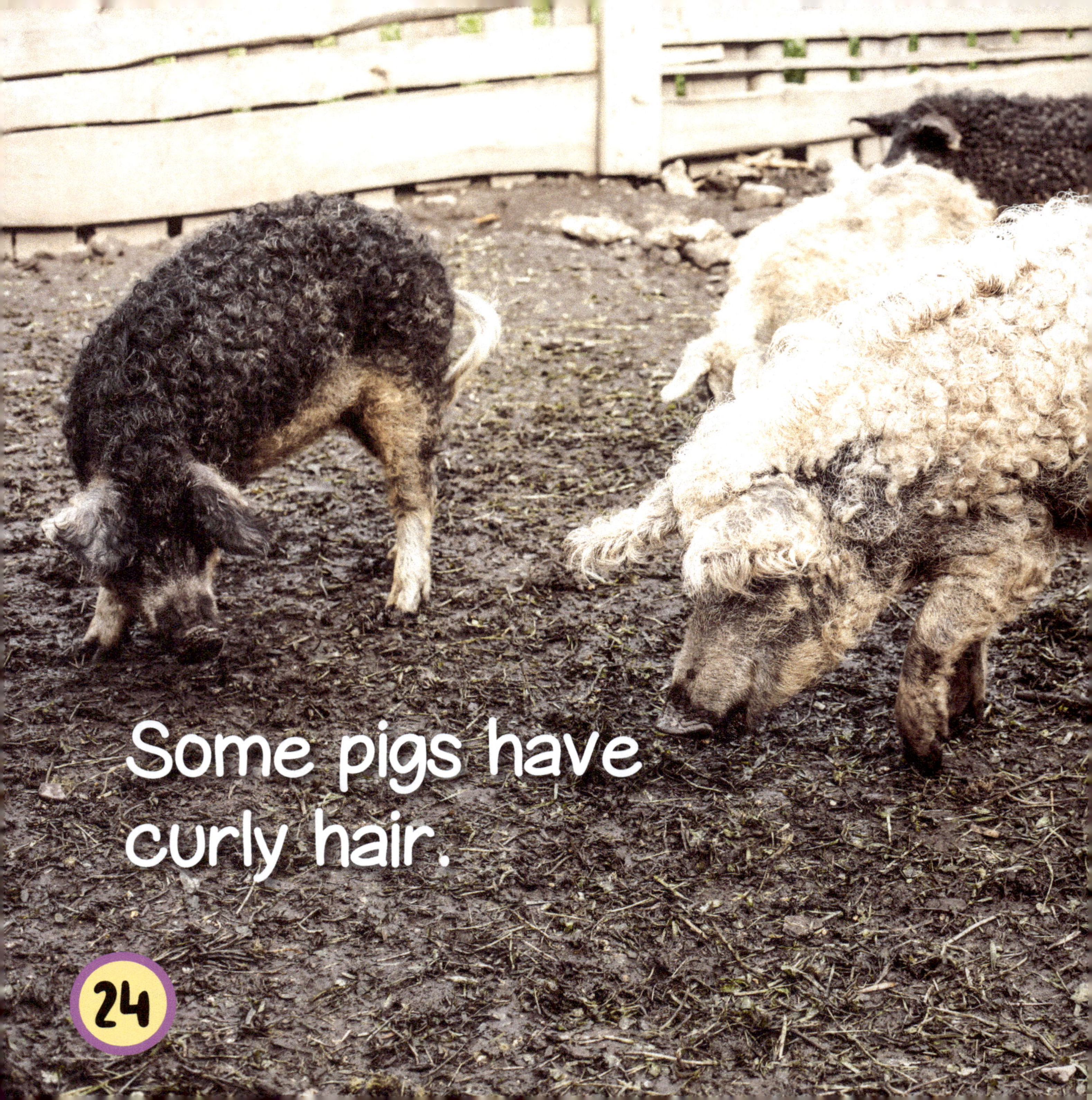

Some pigs have curly hair.

Is your hair curly or straight?

Happy pigs wag their tails.

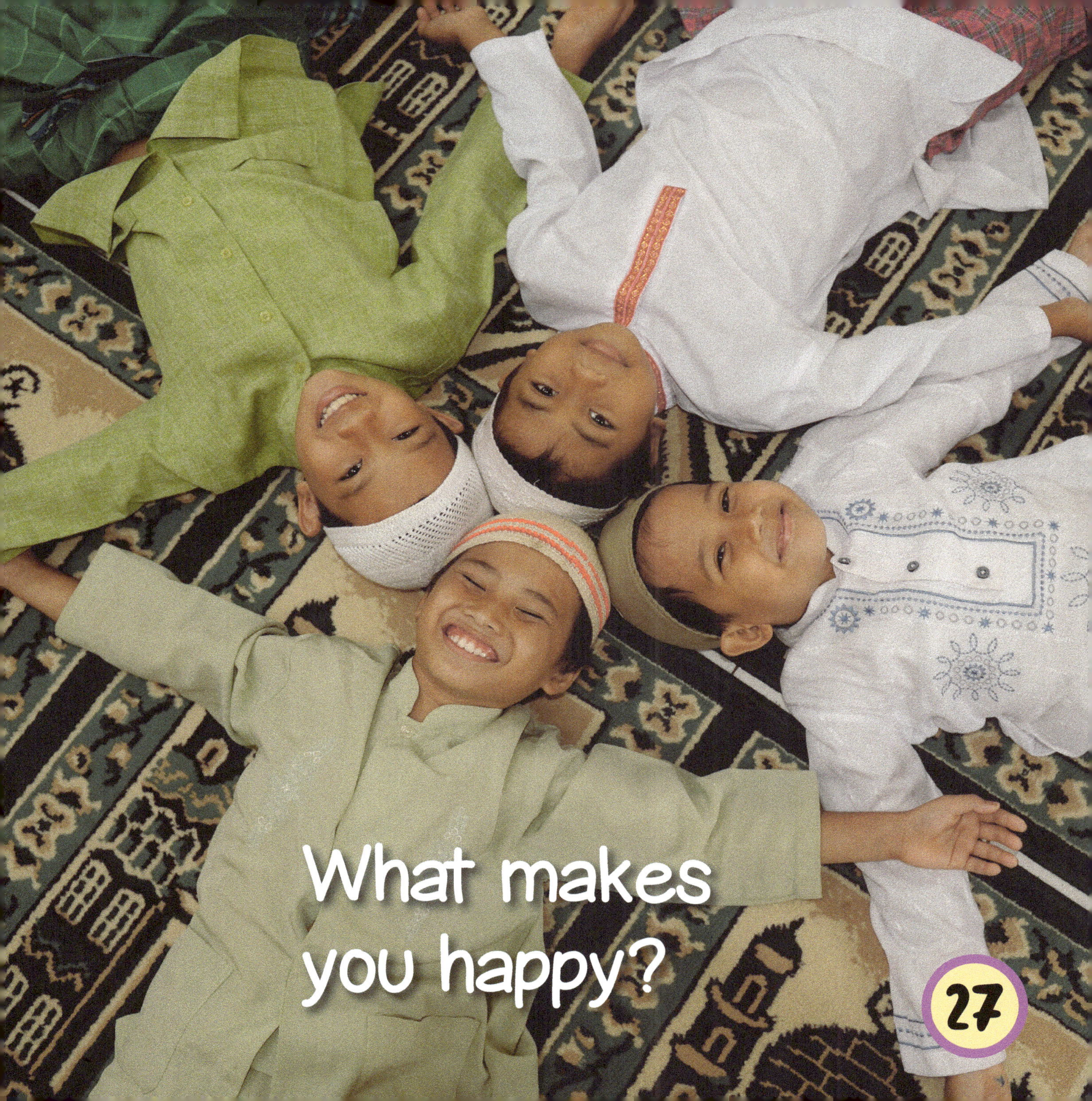

What makes you happy?

Some people keep
pigs as pets.

Do you have a pet?

Pigs are fully grown by the time they are two or three.

Are you fully grown yet?

www.ingramcontent.com/pod-product-compliance
Lightning Source LLC
Chambersburg PA
CBHW041435040426
42452CB00023B/2984